The Kingdom Coalition Manifesto

By Dr. Peter Wyns

The Kingdom Coalition Manifesto $9.95

Copyright ©2020 by Dr. Peter Wyns

To contact the author, please write to the below postal or email address:

Christians For Messiah Ministries
PO Box 36324
Rock Hill, SC 29732

Email: wynsusa@comporium.net

All scriptures taken from the New International Version unless otherwise noted.

Scriptures taken from the Holy Bible, New International Version©

All rights reserved. No part of this publication may be reproduced without prior permission of Christians for Messiah Publishing or Dr. Peter Wyns

Christians For Messiah Publishing edition published 2020

Cover Design by: Ray Austin

Editing by: Jesse Enns, Emma Donnelly

Manufactured in the United States of America by Ingram Spark

ISBN: 978-1-7340341-1-0

Table of Contents

CHAPTER ONE
The Manifesto 1

CHAPTER TWO
Doctrines of Demons 7

CHAPTER THREE
A Kingdom People 17

CHAPTER FOUR
Current Events and Historical Truth 27

CHAPTER FIVE
The Propaganda Machine. 37

CHAPTER SIX
God is Political. 49

CHAPTER SEVEN
The Church, Civil Government, and the Family . . . 59

CHAPTER EIGHT
Church and Israel Solidarity. 69

The Kingdom Coalition Manifesto 77

CHAPTER ONE

The Manifesto

A Public Declaration

A manifesto is a public declaration of policy and aims.

With a broad but brief approach, this document lays out a Kingdom of God Manifesto for all believers. It sets forth a position and a strategy that lines up with the Bible in order to help God's people exist in faith, love and unity. At the end of each chapter a section of the manifesto is presented. At the end of the document, all of the pieces are joined together as one manifesto.

It is called <u>A Kingdom Coalition Manifesto</u> because only the principles of God's kingdom can help us with the current focus on racism, injustice, and other ills in society. Since Christians of every color endeavor to walk in the ways of God, we have formed a coalition to encourage understanding and faith. We call for all believers to stand together in solidarity.

A Biblical Constitution

This manifesto is a Biblical constitution to help God's people initiate social justice, care for the needy, and interact righteously with the community at large. It is a reflection of Biblical truth. It is designed to make us aware of our responsibilities to God, to those within His family, and to the world around us.

By God's grace, we humbly lift these kingdom precepts high, and endeavor to live and walk in these truths for the betterment of the Church and society.

Four Sections

The declaration is presented in four main sections:

1. Challenges Facing God's People
2. Lest We Forget
3. The Biblical Mandate
4. The Call, Commitment and Solidarity of God's Kingdom People.

Those who agree with this manuscript are encouraged to stand alongside one another and demonstrate the undivided community of the redeemed. We, the people of God, are called to stand in sharp contrast to the ways of the world. We are to be a counter culture, set in place by Almighty God to shine brightly in the midst of a dark generation.

"So that you may become blameless and pure, children of God without fault in a crooked and depraved generation, in which you shine like stars in the universe." Phil. 2:15

This manuscript will serve as a guide for believers, and will be a testament to the world of what the Church is and how its members function. It sets forth directives for the Church, civil government and family, so that the peace and gospel of God's kingdom may abound in every place.

On a personal level, it gives Biblical guidelines for service, and encouragement so we might know how to walk with God and to bless one another. This charity must prevail within universal and local expressions of the family of God, and it should be extended far and wide to those outside of the family as well. The love of God is for all who receive it and it must be poured out from God's people as the Holy Spirit enables us to do so.

Manifesto - Section One

We, the people of God, declare that we are one. We are determined to walk together under the Biblical guidelines of the kingdom of God. We will not be divided by physical attributes, culture, or ideology, and together, we will support one another.

We will shine brightly in this world through the gospel of Christ. We embrace social justice, compassion, and grace for all people. Together, we will care for the needy and serve the most vulnerable in our communities.

We declare that our hope is in the Lord Jesus Christ, and that justice in society, and eternal salvation can only be found in Him.

PART ONE

Challenges Facing God's People

CHAPTER TWO

Doctrines of Demons

Responsibilities

The Bible lays out responsibilities for Christians and Jews; it teaches us how to live and gives us a blueprint for God's kingdom. All believers should be in unity concerning these precepts, yet our communities are largely divided in thought and action. True believers desire a common ground of truth and fellowship in accordance with God's word.

People who call themselves Christians vary from devoted disciples to those who are Christian in name only; those people may have no faith or Biblical convictions. We wish that all people would agree to this Manifesto, but we understand that only people of faith will stand in solidarity with us. True disciples, however, realize that they have a responsibility to obey the Lord and line up with the teachings of scripture.

Doctrines of Demons

Today, some anti-Christ voices are persuasive, even to believers. If believers do not know, or are not committed to following God's Word, they can be deceived.

The Bible says, **"In latter times some will abandon the faith and follow deceiving spirits and things taught by demons. Such teachings come through hypocritical liars, whose consciences have been seared with a hot iron."- 1Tim. 4:1-2**

We are warned that believers can be drawn into error by listening to false teachings because they do not know they are listening to the doctrines of demons. The scripture says that false teachings are taught by people who are hypocritical liars, who are defiled and evil. Jesus warned us to be careful what we hear, because it can lead us astray.

"Consider carefully what you hear," he continued. " Mk. 4:24*

Infiltration

The mystery of lawlessness and sin is already in the world. *"For the secret power of lawlessness is already at work." 2Thes. 2:7*

This spiritual power is deceptive and strategic, and has infiltrated God's people. The most effective and far-reaching venue to communicate this anti-Christ teaching is secular universities and even the elementary school systems. These teachings constantly influence young people.

For generations, our youth have been trained, or influenced, by latter-day teachings of Marxism, societal relativism, and intersectionality. Secular universities in the US teach these doctrines of demons, and soon they will be mandatory curriculum. They are now being promoted as diversity classes. Because of recent tensions in society, universities are planning to make all students take at least one diversity class.

Relativism

Relativism is described as, "The doctrine that knowledge, truth, and morality exist in relation to culture, society, or historical context, and are not absolute." - Google Dictionary

To an ungodly person, relativism seems right. It means, however, that there are no unchangeable laws of God for society. Relativism, according to liberals, considers something acceptable if the majority says so. Because of relativism we have legal abortions and gay marriage. Societal preferences overshadow Biblical teachings.

If allowed, this will get much worse. For example, if the majority in society says you can change the sex of your one-year-old child, then, according to relativism it is ok, and you can do it in good conscience. It means that there are no absolute rules.

At some locations in the nation, public school teachers are told they cannot call someone a boy or a girl but just children, because those children may choose, to be identified, as a different sex. This ideology placates sin, immorality and perversion. It is hard to believe, but even some Christians are embracing relativism, citing the old adage - "Live and let live."

As Christians continue to fight back and try to stop this trend they will face strong opposition. The Bible tells us that persecution will come to believers at the end of the age.

"Then you will be handed over to be persecuted..." Mt.24:9

The wages of sin is death and the doctrine of relativism is a doctrine of demons. It is taught enthusiastically, without apology in all secular universities. It is camouflaged under the guise of equality, liberty, and independent thinking. This ideology is convincing to those who are unfamiliar with the Lord and His ways.

Marxism

The second last-days doctrine of devils is Marxism. Marxism is the doctrine that states that capitalism hurts the laborer and needs to be replaced with communism. It says that society should have no classes such as the rich and poor. It forbids religion, personal achievement, and personal wealth (because everything belongs to the state).

Socialism, a product of Marxism, may sound good but the experiment of socialism failed in every nation where it was implemented. It results in tyrannical rule, marshal law, and poverty.

Under socialism, people become addicted to free handouts, and they become lazy. They can never excel or become wealthy. Only those at the top of the system become wealthy because they must be paid to keep controls in place. This practice of corruption goes against the principles of socialism, yet it always happens.

The idea of communism or socialism may seem godly, because everything is shared, but it is a doctrine of demons. It is devised to destroy humanity.

Poverty is not from God; it is a form of demonic destruction. Marxism does not share wealth, it shares poverty. When no one is allowed to prosper there is no money to share.

The Bible does not promote greed, but it does promote prosperity. It teaches a strong work ethic and the resultant blessings of financial abundance. Capitalism is not a perfect system, but it allows for personal promotion, while Marxism or socialism destroys personal ambition, wealth and promotion.

Intersectionality

Here is a third doctrine of demons. It is called intersectionality.

"Intersectionality refers to the social, economic and political ways in which identity-based systems of oppression and privilege connect, overlap and influence one another."
- Google Dictionary

This doctrine of devils says that people are either oppressors or oppressed. This teaching has nothing to do with how people act, but with identity of race, sexual orientation and one's financial disposition. For example, this ridiculous doctrine says, a white male is automatically an oppressor, and a black female is automatically oppressed.

This is called identity politics. Intersectionality states that oppressed people are members of any minority, uneducated, poor, gay people, or anyone who does not have privilege in society. The list of so-called oppressed people is long.

Those who are white, and adhere to the traditional family, wealth and religion are the greatest oppressors by virtue of their prosperity, privilege and identity, regardless of their kindness, generosity or godliness. Intersectionality says they are automatically considered oppressors.

This doctrine encourages hatred, division, polarization and racism. Everyone influenced by this teaching will see people as victims and may lash out with hatred, in the name of social justice, inciting violence and lawlessness.

As the next generation emerges from our secular universities, they come with anti-Christ ideologies. These students are gifted, educated, well-trained leaders of tomorrow. They will fill all of the influential positions in society, and inadvertently, many will be convinced they must lead with an anti-Christ worldview.

This is a challenge for the Christian family and the church, because most parents, pastors, and Sunday School teachers are losing their influence over this generation.

The Power of God

While ungodly agendas are at work in America, so are the great plans of God. The devil and evil people always over-play their hand. As pressure increases, people will wake up. God will shake the nations and the Church. In the midst of the shaking, He will reveal His mighty arm and His wondrous deeds. We will see the Church rise to resist evil, and minister compassion to a world in pain.

Thank God for the power of the Holy Spirit, the salvation of souls through Christ, and the amazing reality of miracles. God will rescue His people by raising up new heroes of the faith. Without that intervention, all would be lost in America and in the world at large.

Manifesto - Section Two

We, the people of God, declare that it is our responsibility to teach our generation the truths of God's word. The task of the Church is not only the salvation of souls, but also the making of disciples, and lifting up a moral standard for the nations to follow.

We proclaim the warnings of the Bible, that seducing spirits and doctrines of demons will come in the last days. Therefore, we oppose the teachings of Marxism, societal relativism, and intersectionality. It is our responsibility to educate our children about these destructive doctrines and to warn all people of these evils. Socialism produces poverty. Relativism inspires sin and immorality. Intersectionality encourages a destructive, polarizing victim mentality. These teachings will destroy a nation. In the name of Jesus, we renounce them.

CHAPTER THREE

A Kingdom People

Kingdom

Another challenge that God's people face is the misunderstanding of the term "Kingdom People." Spiritually speaking, there are only two kingdoms, the kingdom of God's dear Son and the kingdom of darkness. Scripture says, ***"For he has rescued us from the dominion of darkness and brought us into the kingdom of the Son he loves." Col. 1:13***

The Bible tells us repeatedly that bringing God's kingdom to earth is the reason why Jesus came. Jesus prayed to His Father and He taught us to say, *"Your kingdom come, your will be done on earth as it is in heaven." Mt. 6:11*

God's Unshakable Kingdom

A kingdom is the people, government and the domain of a king. The Bible teaches us that in the last days, only the things of Christ's kingdom are unshakable.

We read, *"Once more I will shake not only the earth but also the heavens. The words once more indicate the removing of what can be shaken - that is, created things- so that what cannot be shaken may remain. Therefore, since we are receiving a kingdom that cannot be shaken, let us be thankful, and worship God acceptably with reverence and awe, for our God is a consuming fire." Heb. 12:26-29*

Currently, there is a global shaking due to the Covid-19 pandemic. In addition to the virus, there is a shaking because of social injustice. These shakings highlight the clash of the two kingdoms. The Bible leads us to believe that we are in the latter days, and exhorts us to embrace God's kingdom because it is the only thing that will stand.

The Gospel of the Kingdom

Presently, the church embraces the gospel of salvation but many in the Body do not embrace the gospel of the kingdom.

Scripture says, *"And this gospel of the kingdom will be preached in the whole world as a testimony to all nations, and then the end will come." Mt. 24:14*

Church congregations are essential, but they must come to an understanding of God's kingdom.

We must be unified, for, *"Every kingdom divided against itself will be ruined, and every city or household divided against itself will not stand." Mt. 12:25*

The Church remains divided over doctrines, worship styles, as well as cultural and racial differences. These dynamics separate God's people and segregate us from each other. This polarization cannot last. Adding to all of the external pressures, the Church will suffer persecution. These challenges will draw us together as one people under God.

God's Solution

The Church will soon discover the rising of apostles, prophets, evangelists, pastors and teachers.

This shift is essential because without these leaders we will be a divided people.

The Bible says, *"It was he who gave some to be apostles, some to be prophets, some to be evangelists, and some to be pastors and teachers, to prepare God's people for works of service, so that the body of Christ may be built up until we all reach unity in the faith and in the knowledge of the Son of God and become mature, attaining to the whole measure of the fullness of Christ. Then we will no longer be infants, tossed back and forth by the waves, and blown here and there by every wind of teaching and by the cunning and craftiness of men in their deceitful scheming. Instead, speaking the truth in love, we will in all things grow up into him who is the Head, that is Christ." Eph. 4:11-15*

Tossed Like Children

Sadly, many believers are like infants, being tossed around by winds of deceitful teaching. For the most part, the church is not trained to deal with the tribulations released on the world. Many Christians are fearful, aimless, and depressed, and are becoming even more divided as personal ambitions rise.

God shows us the answer to this dilemma - the activation of His government. The task of leaders is to equip the people of God for service and guide them into unity, faith, spiritual understanding and maturity.

The Renewal of the Mind

A new mindset is required, and it involves sanctification. Sanctification is the work of the Holy Spirit in us.

This is the on-going plan of salvation. *". . . continue to work out your salvation with fear and trembling, for it is God who works in you to will and to act according to his good purpose." Phi. 2:12-13*

Christians are under the New Covenant, and with this provision, the Holy Spirit becomes our teacher (see Heb. 8:10-12). When we give all that we are to God, He promises to show us His will and transform us by the renewing of our minds (see Rom. 12:1-2). This renewal will change our ideology, our attitudes and our behavior.

Our theology produces our ideology.
Our ideology produces our attitudes.
Our attitudes produce our behavior.

As the world is shaken, God will change our thinking and our behavior. The fear of God will come upon His people; this will cause His Church to cry out for help. Many Christians will rededicate their lives to God. Then, the Lord will meet us at a deeper level and begin to renew our minds. New behavior will be released in the Christian community as our attitudes and doctrines shift. Then the kingdom of God will become visible.

Emboldened Leaders

The Bible uses the example of the lion and the lamb to describe the power and gentleness of Christ. He is the Lion from the tribe of Judah, and also the Lamb of God who takes away the sins of the world.

This gives us a picture of Christ's kingdom activity. His people are sent forth as both lambs and lions, to represent Him in the world (see Lk. 10:3,10-15).

Church leaders are called to be kingdom-of-God leaders. They must learn to lead and equip God's people with the qualities of the lion and the lamb; they must lead with courage, authority and power like a lion, but also be gentle and compassionate like the Lamb of God.

The Kingdom Challenge

When we consider the theological shift needed in the church, we realize the huge challenge before us. The Body needs to align itself with God's Word, be sanctified and emboldened to present God's truth to the world.

Manifesto - Section Three

We, the people of God, humble ourselves under the mighty hand of God. We bow before Jesus our king and embrace His government in our lives. We receive and look to the ministry of true apostles, prophets, evangelists, pastors and teachers as part of God's government on earth.

We present our lives to God for sanctification and the renewal of our minds so we may be transformed in our thinking and behavior.

We join together as kingdom-of-God people to preach this gospel of the kingdom in all the world. We declare that we are God's family, and we pledge our allegiance to His kingdom.

PART TWO

Lest We Forget

CHAPTER FOUR

Current Events and Historical Truth

A Volcanic Situation

At present, it seems that the world has been turned upside down. In just a few short months, we have experienced a viral pandemic and a polarizing movement focused on racism in America. Racism is wicked, but this movement has produced violence, anarchy, and political strife.

It seems that our black and white communities are becoming more hostile toward each other as each puts forth their perspectives on racial injustice.

This is exacerbated by shutdowns of businesses across the country, mandated by government leaders due to fears of the Covid-19 virus. It feels as though a fuse has been lit, and a worldwide eruption is looming on the horizon. Every social norm is changing. It began in January, and as I write, we are only half way through 2020. Everything is being shaken.

The Federal Election

This volatile climate has intensified because of the election that is months away. Political policies are more extreme and radical ideologies aim to change America at its core. Some of the changes even threaten to eradicate America's Biblical foundations.

Across the nation, people are worried. Some say that the erosion of America's history and culture is the present day trauma. Others say that Covid-19 is the biggest problem we are facing. Still others claim that the main problem on the streets of America is social injustice!

It is rooted in our history of slavery, and continues into present day racism. But there is a final group that believes the strife in our land is spiritual. It is an anti-Christ spirit that wants to destroy every vestige of spirituality and godly virtue in America.

The nation will soon face an important election. Many believe that America will spiral out of control, depending on the outcome of the 2020 election. The nation is so polarized that this election will bring relief and elation to the winners but immense sorrow, grief, and trepidation to the losers.

Slavery, Racism and the Police

One of the firestorms rocking America is the focus on slavery and racism. The horrors of slavery were evident at the founding of the nation, and racism is still present hundreds of years later. Unarmed black men and women have been killed by police officers, and the world is enraged by alleged, systematic injustice against the black community.

As a result, many in the USA refuse to pledge allegiance to the flag or honor our nation, and seek to rewrite American history. Statues have been toppled, government buildings have been vandalized, and police officers have been attacked from the very community they serve. Some abuse against officers has even come from government leaders who refuse support law enforcement efforts.

Protests have turned into violent riots in some major cities throughout the land. Rioters have burned buildings and destroyed businesses, even shutting down entire city blocks. News networks have filmed widespread looting, violence, and destruction. Police have been told to stand down and the crime and murder rate has escalated in these cities. Anarchy is seen in the states and cities where progressive mayors and governors are sympathetic to these protesters and rioters. They have told the police to let these anarchists have their way.

Many of these anarchists are anti-God, anti country, anti-Church, anti-Christian, anti-baby-in-the womb, anti-Israel, anti-traditional family, anti-founding fathers, anti-flag, anti-government, and anti-Christ.

The Church should come together and make a unified statement for peace and godliness in America. It is time for kingdom brothers and sisters to stand as one in the purposes of God.

Atrocities Everywhere

One of the reasons that some are anti-flag, anti-founding fathers, and anti-America is because most founding fathers had slaves. Each of us, however, can find examples of horror with our own ancestors, no matter where we come from.

The Mongols had their bloody hoards, as did the Chinese, Japanese, and Koreans. The Russians perpetrated bloodthirsty massacres and Europeans had their violent crusades and tortuous regimes. The hands of the North American Indians were covered in blood, as were the native peoples of Central and South America, sacrificing a thousand men a day, until blood ran like a river down their pyramids. In Africa, tribes butchered neighboring tribes and sold them as slaves. Muslims invaded nation after nation, decapitating any who would not covert. Every nation and people around the world has a history of demonic evil. Somewhere, in your personal ancestry atrocities existed.

Jesus said, **"Let any one of you who is without sin be first to throw a stone." Jn. 8:7**

Included with such rampant bloodshed and abuse, the horror of slavery was everywhere around the world. Human atrocities are still happening today and we should do all we can to stop it.

Burning the Flag

If we burn America's flag because of the atrocities present in its beginnings, we should burn every flag in every nation and destroy every government around the world. A misguided effort to reform America by cancelling its culture will result in a far worse situation than what we have now.

That is not the answer to social reform. Lawless anarchism will result in a repeat of the bloody French Revolution, the horrors of the Spanish Inquisition, Nazism, and murderous Communism. Only in Christ, and the Bible, will we find reformation that can heal the wounded and produce blessings for all.

Some Christians say that they do not agree with the actions and premise of this riotous movement, but they believe social justice is being produced by it, so the end justifies the means. The Bible, however, warns us against that kind of thinking. It clearly teaches that sweet water cannot come from a poisoned well, and good fruit cannot come from an evil tree (see Jas. 3:11 and Mt. 7:17-18).

Current Events and Historical Truth

The riotous movements on the streets of America are disingenuous. They care little about black lives and only about their anti-Christ agenda. If you are a person of color, and you are a Christian who is against abortion and the expansion of the gay agenda, then you are their enemy. Once they have accomplished their present goals they will persecute and attack anyone who does not agree with them.

Reformation

People want social justice and reform. The Bible teaches what is right and wrong, and how righteousness can be achieved in the land. Historically speaking, the Church has experienced great reformations. Powerful shifts in Church theology and activity changed the politics of nations. We are in desperate need of a new reformation in the Church. When it arrives, it will change the world.

Manifesto - Section Four

We, the Church, take a firm stand against social injustice and mob violence. We renounce all anarchistic behavior in America and reject leaders who side with such destructive ways.

The Kingdom Coalition Manifesto

We thank God for birthing our nation. We declare that God established our union with the help of great leaders and gave us a divinely inspired Constitution.

We thank Almighty God for the time allotted to us as a nation, for our borders, our flag and our founding fathers. Because America was founded by God on Christian principles, we gladly pledge allegiance to the flag of the United States of America.

We abhor slavery and repent on behalf of the nation for our participation in it. We also cry out against present day social injustice.

Let it be known that we are thankful for our police officers but detest the actions of those who have wrongfully killed unarmed people of color. We call for ongoing racial reform in the nation. We declare our thanks to God for all first responders who serve our communities with valor and godly grace.

We stand in solidarity with all brothers and sisters in Christ, especially those who fear being singled out, abused or killed, when they have done nothing worthy of death. We ask the Lord for safety in our streets, and for grace to remove fear from our minority communities.

We declare that only the Lord Jesus Christ can heal our land, and we embrace Biblical teachings as the only way to reformation and healing in America.

CHAPTER FIVE

The Propaganda Machine

Propaganda

Through the years, evil has periodically bulldozed its way forward. It gained momentum as wicked men manipulated people into ungodly conformity. They controlled nations with slanderous and deceptive propaganda.

Propaganda is, "information, especially of a biased or misleading nature, used to promote or publicize a particular cause or point of view." - Google Dictionary

Before an evil leader or group can take control of a nation, they must influence the hearts of the people. Using selective and false information they present a biased perspective. This is achieved by controlling the channels of communication so that people only see what the deceiver wants them to see.

Jesus told us to be careful what we hear (see Mk. 4:24). People tend to believe what they hear, especially when it is constantly repeated and made to sound persuasive.

An effective propaganda campaign will silence opposing viewpoints, leaving people with only the campaign's ideology. It will always present its opponent in an evil or bad light, and never speak good of that opponent.

Ideally, the mainstream news media should report its news with unbiased political neutrality, but this is not the case in America today. Depending on the TV or radio channel, the audience will get an opposite perspective. These opposite reports reveal that at least one of the communicators is using evil propaganda. Just like it happened during wicked seasons of past history, it is happening in America right now. Some media outlets are allowing evil propaganda: we call it Fake News.

A History of Propaganda

Propaganda was used effectively in ancient Rome under Nero and Constantine. In more modern times, Nazi Germany, Communist Russia, Communist China, and dozens of other nations around the world use or used propaganda to fuel their agendas. For example, in Nazi Germany, the media was so controlled that no one was allowed to speak against the government. Media outlets blamed the Jews for all of the problems in society, and depicted them as inferior creatures with greedy dispositions.

The next step was to fire all Jews from their jobs and shutdown all of their businesses. Eventually, any individuals who opposed the ruling ideology were imprisoned or murdered. In time, millions of Jews, and all dissidents were slaughtered.

Those who use the propaganda machine control the media. They endeavor to eliminate any voice of disagreement. Once freedom of speech is gone, the removal of other freedoms will follow.

Persecution in America

It is hard to believe that this could happen in America, but as it happened in other nations, within the last one hundred years, it can occur here. Without Christ, the human heart can be desperately wicked.

In the days of Fake News, anything can be slanted, selective or false. If it is evil, manipulative and controlling it is a form of witchcraft. Witchcraft occurs when one entity dominates the thinking or the spirit of another using deception, manipulation or violence. Most news networks in America are using evil propaganda, and it is not difficult to identify it.

Propaganda Right Now

In present-day America, propaganda is running at an intense level. For example, conservatives know of many good things that President Trump has done for the people of America. Over the past three and a half years there have been many positive, godly policies put in place by him, however, the mainstream news media refuses to publish any of those achievements. Their presentation is always focused on slandering and destroying President Trump. This is blatant propaganda, and it is seen every day in America.

Strategic Propaganda

Propaganda is being force-fed to the people of America through the narrow canyon of media outlets. It gushes forth like boiling water from underground geysers and spews forth from three main sources - the Democratic Party, secular universities, and liberal news outlets. The book of Revelation speaks of this happening in the last days.

It says, *"Then from his mouth the serpent spewed water like a river, to overtake the woman and sweep her away in the torrent." Rev. 12:15*

The serpent is the devil, the river is the propaganda machine, and the woman represents the people of God. Reading further, the scripture says that the devil's propaganda machine fails and the people of God are rescued.

It should be illegal for the news media and universities to present biased ideology, but it is not. These institutions are political to the core and almost exclusively liberal. They continually push a lawless, anti-Christ agenda and hate the ways of the Lord, which interfere with their ideology.

Goodness Still Abounds

There is one human force of spiritual strength left in America; it is the Church. Only those who embrace the values of God's Word will consistently do all of the following;

1. Resist abortion
2. Promote traditional family values
3. Help feed and shelter the disadvantaged
4. Support God's chosen people Israel
5. Encourage entrepreneurial prosperity
6. Embrace patriotism
7. Care for minorities
8. Promote safety and justice
9. Insist on responsible education
10. Help people of other nations
11. Fight for freedom of speech
12. Uphold the Constitution and the flag

Besides the Church, another group that fights for goodness in America is our conservative news sources. The Fox News network and others, along with some conservative radio hosts, promote similar moral views to that of traditional Christianity.

Fox News, reports on community care that is extended from the Christian community. It airs testimonies of people who praise God for rescuing them from disaster and speaks of people who have come to faith in Christ.

Without God using Fox News, it is difficult to imagine how support for this nation, for our president and for the promotion of a Christian worldview, would be communicated in America.

A third place of Biblical strength and godly communication in the USA is found in our Christian universities. These universities enable students to receive the education they need without the propaganda of progressive ideology. Although the numbers universities and their enrollment is much smaller than that of the secular liberal universities, they are still influencing many young people with a godly worldview and encouraging them to live as bright shining lights in the nation. I encourage all families in the USA to send their children to Christian universities.

May the Church, the conservative media networks, and Christian universities become more numerous and effective. Let the word of the Lord resound over the airwaves to reach every corner of the country.

Manifesto - Section Five

We, the People of God, take our stand against lying fake news and propaganda. We resist the selective, slanderous bias of evil communication. We expose it as a form of witchcraft and resist its agenda and the evil spirit behind it.

We resist every political ideology and movement that does not stand for the life of the unborn child, the family, the Church, the poor, social justice for all people and for the support of Israel, who are God's chosen people. We declare that our voting, at government elections, will reflect these values as much as possible.

We declare that poverty is a curse and encourage all political leaders to establish opportunities for all who will work hard so they can prosper financially.

We declare that the truth will set people free. As such, we thank God for our president, our Christian universities and for news networks that communicate truth and promote godly lifestyles.

We thank Almighty God for believers who serve in the political arena, and for believers who report accurate news and influence society for justice and godliness. We thank God for Bible-based education in America at every level, especially in places of higher learning.

We declare our thanks to God for all first responders who serve our communities with valor and godly grace.

PART THREE

The Biblical Mandate

CHAPTER SIX

God is Political

A Challenge to Pastors

Although most pastors in America follow the example of scripture as best they can, they might be oblivious to some things that are clearly outlined in the Bible. I want to call the ministers in America to be more Christ-like, not just in character, but also in the exercise of practical and public ministry. Jesus was very outspoken about society and toward those who influenced it. In that sense, He was very political. We can only be like Him as He empowers us, but I challenge all ministers to ask the Lord to give them courage and faith to be more outspoken. The Church needs you.

Warn the Congregation

The Bible tells the ministers of God that it is their solemn responsibility to warn people of approaching danger. If ministers do not do this, then the blood of the people will be on their hands.

Right now, America is in a dangerous place. The sword of destruction is coming against this nation and pastors should speak out and warn their congregations.

Look at these verses. *"When I bring the sword against the land, and the people choose one of their men and make him their watchman, and he sees the sword coming against the land and blows the trumpet to warn the people, then if anyone hears the trumpet but does not take warning and the sword comes and takes his life, his blood will be on his own head. Since he heard the sound of the trumpet but did not take warning, his blood will be on his own head. If he had taken warning, he would have saved himself. But if the watchman sees the sword coming but does not blow the trumpet to warn the people and the sword comes and takes the life of one of them, that man will be taken away because of his sin, but I will hold the watchman accountable for his blood. Son of man, I have made you a watchman for the house of Israel; so hear the word I speak and give them warning from me." Eze. 33:2-7*

The Johnson Law

It is our religious duty to warn the people that the government does not rightfully have authority to take free speech from pastors. Regardless of the laws of the land, it is an edict from God that His ministers must sound the trumpet and warn the people when the enemy is approaching. The Johnson amendment is an attack against the free speech of pastors.

"The Johnson Amendment is a provision in the U.S. tax code... that prohibits all 501(c)(3) non-profit organizations from endorsing or opposing political candidates." - Google Wikipedia

The Johnson Law is unconstitutional; the first amendment to the constitution sets in place freedom of religion and freedom of speech without reprisals from the government.

More than being unconstitutional, the Johnson Law is unbiblical. If any group or person in society should be free to lead, give direction and influence the culture, it is the Church and the Christian pastor.

On many occasions, the early apostles preached what God told them to preach, even when those in power forbade them to do so.

They said, ***"We must obey God rather than men!" Acts 5:2***

Should we obey God or man? When conflicted, the apostles only obeyed the Lord. Since when does civil government rule over the edicts of heaven?

Things have recently changed; the Church has a new friend in the White House. President Trump signed a document giving greater liberty to churches to espouse political views and recommend political candidates. Pastors should give clear instructions and strong suggestions to their congregations concerning the nation's political future. This is a matter of faith and it is a matter of national righteousness. Remember - righteousness exults a nation.

Jesus Criticized National Leaders Publically

It is a common error to say that Jesus did not preach against evil political leaders. Matthew's gospel says, ***"Then Jesus said to the crowds and to his disciples. "The teachers of the law and the Pharisees sit in Moses' seat. So you must obey them... But do not do what they do." Mt.23:1-2.***

Jesus calls out the evil leaders of Israel before a huge public gathering. It should be noted that the Pharisees were part of the Sanhedrin Council. As such, they made civil laws that the Jews had to obey. They had political power to punish those who did not obey and, at various seasons, they even had the right to order the death penalty for violators.

Jesus spoke aggressively against the ungodly political leaders of His day. Matthew 23 records His indictment. If we did not know that it was Jesus speaking, we would say that the speaker was rough, or rude or too bold; certainly it could not be Jesus speaking, but it *was* Him.

What Jesus Said in Public About the Political Pharisees

1. They don't practice what they preach.
2. They put heavy loads on others that they are not willing to bear.
3. Everything they do is just done for men to see.

4. They love to show off and to only draw attention to themselves.
5. Seven times in these thirty-seven verses, Jesus calls them Hypocrites.
6. They shut the kingdom of God in men's faces, not allowing them to enter.
7. They refuse to enter the kingdom of God themselves.
8. They go to great lengths to make converts and turn them into sons of hell.
9. They are blind guides who lead the blind.
10. They are full of greed.
11. They are full of self-indulgence.
12. They are whitewashed tombs.
13. They are full of dead men's bones and everything that is unclean.
14. They paint a good picture outside, but inside they are full of wickedness.
15. Their forefathers were evil.
16. They are murderers.
17. They are snakes.
18. They are people abusers.
19. They are guilty of shedding innocent blood.
20. They adamantly refuse to receive the grace of God.

Jesus the Lion

The twenty bold accusations listed above would be slanderous if they were not true. This is a demonstration of spiritual, political fervor that required great courage and a huge release of unbridled truth. Jesus held nothing back.

His list of accusations is not politically correct, and His example is one that all Christian ministers should follow.

God Hates Some Things

These portions of scripture will be troublesome to some Christians, but we need the teachings and application of God's word in our lives. God is Love and as such, He hates some things and some people because they are evil.

"There are six things the Lord hates, seven that are detestable to Him: haughty eyes, a lying tongue, hands that shed innocent blood, a heart that devises wicked schemes, feet that are quick to rush into evil, a false witness who pours out lies and a person who stirs up conflict in the community." Pro. 6:16-19

As a minister of God, I hate racism, the KKK, the white supremacist movement, Fake news, the abortionist industry that sheds innocent blood, corrupt politicians, community troublemakers, arrogant pride, serial murderers, and the anti-Christ spirit.

Fight for What is Right

Soon, Americans will elect our next president and House of Representatives. We should vote for life for the unborn child, conservative Supreme Court judges, freedom of speech in the Church, prison reform, support of Israel, a strong economy to fight poverty, freedom of school choice, a better and more prosperous life for minorities, secure borders, individual prosperity, protection against riots, crime and violence, Constitutional originalism, patriotism, and for Judeo-Christian standards of morality to be promoted in the nation.

As a watchman on the wall, I warn you not to vote for ungodly policies. The Bible teaches that curses come as a result of murdering the innocent, hurting the disadvantaged, promoting sexual perversions, injustice, corruption, persecuting Israel, and occult involvement. Curses are a result of wicked sins and they come to families, individuals and nations.

This election is a spiritual, Church matter. The Church has the strength to be in-step with God and lead us forward to a better, more godly nation.

I also ask all pastors to be bold and speak up for the children, the people of God, this nation and for the Lord. Influence your congregation with strong, decisive, political advice.

Manifesto - Section Six

We, the people of God, declare that this nation was created for God's eternal purpose. We are deeply concerned about the welfare of America and the advancement of its Christian principles. In that sense, we declare ourselves to be a political people.

We are determined to fight for the blessings of God to remain in America. We follow the example of Jesus who spoke against ungodly leadership in Israel, and we shall do the same in America.

We declare that our help comes from the Lord. We do not rely on the efforts of man to give us salvation or ultimate security.

By God's grace, we aim to take the high ground of government. We will be political and vote for God-inspired leaders who will enact righteous policies and governance.

The Kingdom Coalition Manifesto

We proclaim that God has blessed this nation and will continue to bless it in the future. As we will diligently seek the Lord and serve Him, we are assured of His blessings over America for generations to come.

CHAPTER SEVEN

The Church, Civil Government, and the Family

A Larger Perspective

As kingdom-of-God people, we understand that God's kingdom reaches beyond our Church services. To Him, there is no difference between the secular and the spiritual. All things belong to Him and will be ruled by Him. The earth is the Lord's and all who dwell in it. He is Lord of the Church, the streets, the political arena and our homes.

There are three God-given institutions on earth: the family, the Church and civil government. Each institution plays a vital role in the provision of God's care over individual lives and the corporate community. When functioning as designed, each institution's responsibilities overlap so that complete care of the community and individual is met. When any of these institutions fail, the other two attempt to cover for the shortfall, however, the covering and care will lack the full provision intended by the Lord.

Like the three branches of government in the USA, (the executive, judicial and legislative branches), the three institutions (family, government and Church) act as a balance and check to each other. Here are the responsibilities of each institution.

The Family

An ideal, God-ordained family consists of one man, one woman and their children, if they have any. In some cases, there may be a one-parent family. The Lord gives special grace for that parent to minister His love and provision.

The Church, Civil Government, and the Family

The family is an expression of intimate love and care. God compares the husband and wife to Christ and His Church. Spouses are called to lay down their lives for each other, to watch over the concerns and needs of one another, and their children.

This care is especially important for the children, who are the most vulnerable members of the family. Children are a gift from God; they are His inheritance, to be raised for His glory. Parents do not own children; they steward and train them to be outstanding members of God's family. All children are designed by God for greatness. Parents pour the best of their love and goodness into their children so that each generation will be better than the one before it.

Responsibilities of care for children involve great focus and vigilance. It is the primary responsibility of parents to protect their children from any kind of harm. That includes physical, spiritual, sexual or social harm of any kind.

It is also the responsibility of parents to oversee their children's education. When they are young, children are mentally vulnerable and parents must teach them to have a godly worldview. This includes good manners, practical skills, the precepts and values of the Bible, and a powerful faith and dependence on God.

Parents are also responsible for sheltering and feeding their children, however, the Church and government may help if a family comes upon hard times. That is God's provision.

Each family should be unified as a force for good in the community, in the Church and in the nation.

The Church

The Church is designed by God. When functioning properly, it represents the larger family of God's people. It is the setting for corporate worship, training and instruction. The Lord Himself will be present through His Holy Spirit, as His people meet and worship Him. In that place of worship, God releases faith, prophecy, apostolic wisdom, governmental leadership and healing.

The Church is also a testing ground for our submission to God and our humility before one another. Both of these dynamics are required for disciples of Christ; none of us should be an island unto ourselves.

The Church should provide godly teaching and instruction to the family, and be God's voice to civil government, the community, the nation and the world.

The Church, Civil Government, and the Family

The Church is the training ground for all things spiritual. It is a community of love, righteousness, joy, peace, miracles, increased faith and supernatural signs and wonders.

Part of the equipping of the saints is the impartation and release of faith for miraculous signs and wonders. The Church believes in miracles. The people of God believe in supernatural healings, casting out of demons, and supernatural answers to prayers of faith. We are not those people who, in the last days, have a form of religion but deny the power of God (see 1Tim. 3:2). Jesus told His disciples that when He cast out demons, they should know that the kingdom of God has come (see Lk. 11:20).

Paul said, *"My message and my preaching were not with wise and persuasive words, but with a demonstration of the Spirit's power." 1Cor.2:4*

Deeper levels of spiritual impartation and equipping will only be discovered, released and exercised as we receive God's provision through the Church. It is the pillar and ground of the truth, the fullness of Him who fills all in all (see Eph. 1: 22-23).

The Church is God's family.

Civil Government

The third God-given and God-established institution is civil government. We are called to pray for our government.

"I urge, then, first of all, that petitions, prayers, intercession and thanksgiving be made for all people- for kings and all those in authority, that we may live peaceful and quiet lives in all godliness and holiness." 1Tim.2:1-2

This is a power-packed scripture that highlights the responsibilities of civil government. This is what it teaches us:

1. We are to pray and give thanks for government leaders.
2. Federal and local authorities must serve the people.
3. They are to enforce law, order and security.
4. They must maintain peace and quiet so we may live godly lives.
5. They are to provide a setting for the development of holiness.

Government responsibilities include: protection for individuals, families and communities, from all enemies, foreign and domestic. In our world it also includes the management of the environment and community infrastructure.

Laws and policies must be decided and mandated continually for the well being of all law-abiding people. This is a challenge because consideration must be given to all of the diversity in our communities.

Without embracing the values of family, the Bible and the Church, it is impossible for those who hold governmental authority to lead appropriately. For example, many laws, such as the right to have an abortion, are a violation against God and against humanity. That law exists because those in authority ignored the teachings of the Bible.

Families, the church, and godly politicians must work hard to undo evil laws in the land and bring godly reformation to America.

Manifesto - Section Seven

We, the people of God, recognize the three institutions that He has given. They are the family, the Church and civil government.

We declare that, along with the hosts of heaven, the kingdom of God includes these three institutions, and each is called to rule righteously. Each has a God-given authority over their area of influence, and we will strengthen, uphold and pray for them.

We believe in the Biblical model for family: one man, woman and children if they have any. We also understand that a godly family may have only one parent.

We believe in the community of God's holy Church, in spiritual worship, submitting to one another in the fear of God, and in miracles and supernatural answers to prayer.

We declare that the power of God is with us today to perform supernatural signs and wonders. We believe that God is good, His mercies are everlasting and His faithfulness extends to all generations. God's grace and provisions are all we need. We do not frustrate the grace of God but receive His blessings with thanksgiving (see Gal. 2:21).

We will do our part to support and reform each of these three institutions as needed. When any of them violate the designs of heaven, so as to serve the kingdom of darkness, we will not be silent, but will expose the hidden things of darkness, and by God's grace, aim to enact a righteous resolve.

PART FOUR

Kingdom Manifesto Solidarity

CHAPTER EIGHT

Church and Israel Solidarity

A United Universe

We will talk about the importance of Israel, and why they should be included in this coalition at the end of this chapter, but let us begin with the solidarity of the Church.

The Lord our God is One, and His great plan is to make the universe one, under His rule. Division, alienation and segregation are not for God's people. Still, we the family of God, do not flow together as we should. This truth rises before us like a formidable mountain that we must cross. Our division is an affront to God's design and a hindrance to the release of blessings.

He has made us different. We come from different cultures, have different physical appearances, speak different languages and have different personalities and sensitivities. None of us see all of the truth, yet we rightly contend for the parts that we do see. Sometimes, our understanding and sensitivities cause us to offend each other. We separate ourselves like estranged members of a dysfunctional family. How can the people of God's kingdom work together, encourage one another and stand together in solidarity?

Recognizing Spiritual authority

Only senior spiritual leaders can bring God's people together as a unified force. In the time of the early Church, the senior elders and apostles met to discuss the issues of God's kingdom (see Acts 13 and 15). Some theologians call them the five-fold ministry leaders. These leaders included apostles, prophets, evangelists, pastors and Bible teachers.

Today, in some denominations, these leaders may be called by different names. They may be men or women, but they function as spiritual leaders over God's people.

In the New Testament, all believers met from house to house, ministering to one another and breaking bread. It was only the five-fold ministers, however, who could congregate the people for unified governmental purpose. In the first days of the early church, it happened on the temple mount (see Acts 3:11 and 5:13) but as persecution erupted, the gospel of the kingdom spread far and wide to cities and nations beyond Jerusalem.

When Philip went to Samaria and Barnabas went to Antioch, each of them saw a powerful move of God. Then, they called for other senior leaders to come and bring more anointing for ministry breakthrough and revival (see Acts 8 and 11).

Solidarity

Without embracing spiritual fathers, mothers and five-fold ministry leaders, the solidarity of God's people will be delayed. In recent years, some leaders have led significant events around the nation and many are networking as the Lord brings them together. These apostolic connections must continue to develop as the Holy Spirit orchestrates God's end-time agenda.

In days to come, chosen fathers and mothers will carry kingdom government, and the people of God will recognize it. The Church is looking for leadership and a rallying point for the flow of God's purpose. The united government of these leaders will bring unity and purpose to the Body of Christ.

Once leaders are comfortable with each other and begin to honor one another, they will provide pathways for congregations to connect. Then, the world will see one Church, and the people of God will come into solidarity.

A Coming Together

The Lord has begun connecting Church leaders in various cities. Soon, more of them will meet for apostolic and prophetic synergism. The Lord will give marching orders to gather His people. Individual Churches will still have their congregations, yet will see themselves as part of the city-wide Church. Then, the Church will be more effective in the nation; reformation and revival will follow.

The Issue of Israel

In addition to Church solidarity, the subject of God's chosen people and the land of Israel must be addressed. Most of the Bible focuses on the Jewish people and we cannot circumnavigate the importance of their role in God's great plan. Their role is not simply a matter of history; the Lord has them destined for purpose in the future.

When Jesus returns, His feet will land on the Mount of Olives in Jerusalem, and right now, in heaven, Jesus is referred to the Lion from the tribe of Judah. They are part of God's kingdom plan, and in the millennium, they will be central to His rule over the earth.

At that time, Americans and people of other nations will go up to Jerusalem to worship the Lord Jesus as He sits on the throne in Jerusalem (see Isa. 2:2-5 and Zec. 14:16). The Jews who have become disciples of Christ will serve Him in a special way at that time. Therefore, we cannot think of a kingdom-of-God coalition and leave them out of the equation.

At the founding of the United States, and more so since 1948, God has connected us with the Jewish people. Our future as a nation is linked with the land of Israel and His purposes with His chosen people.

All Christians should bless the Jews and pray for the peace of Jerusalem, for their spiritual promotion and their full salvation through Jesus the Messiah. We should agree that they are God's chosen people and that He has a special role for them in His kingdom. Whoever blesses them will be blessed. We look for ways the Lord will connects us with them until we are in walking in solidarity.

This Manifesto

This manifesto is a call for God's people to be unified. We ask for a commitment from all believers to seek and find common ground. The next chapter is the manifesto. If you agree with it, please let us know by sending us an acknowledgment with your name and contact information, that we may stand together for the purposes of God.

We trust that this manifesto will find its way into cities across America and be a model for other nations around the world to follow.

Perhaps a more complete document will be written in the future; for now, I pray that the Lord will connect us. We dream of this.

"When the LORD restored the fortunes of Zion, we were like those who dreamed. Our

mouths were filled with laughter, out tongues with songs of joy. Then it was said among the nations, "The LORD has done great things for them."" Ps.126:1-2

Manifesto - Section Eight

We, the people of God, declare that the Father, Son, and Holy Spirit are One, and that the Lord will one day unify everything under His government.

We declare that the Church is one in Christ. We are one body (see 1Cor. 12) yet we long for the practical manifestation of that unity. We confess that the Church does not yet function as a family, but in time it will.

By God's grace, we humble ourselves, receive His government and come into unity as best we can. Together, we move forward in ministry to see revival in the nations.

We desire the joining of the Lord with other Christians for righteous networking in the body of Christ. We listen for and respond with obedience to God's purpose over America and the nations of the world. We rally together under the banner of Christ.

We declare that the Jewish people are God's chosen people. We agree that the Lord has a unique end-time purpose for them. We bless them and pray for the peace of Jerusalem and for their salvation through Jesus the Messiah. We, the Church, pray for the complete fulfillment of the call of God over the Jews and over the land of Israel.

The Kingdom Coalition Manifesto

We, the people of God, declare that we are one. We are determined to walk together under the Biblical guidelines of the kingdom of God. We will not be divided by physical attributes, culture, or ideology, and together, we will support one another.

We will shine brightly in this world through the gospel of Christ. We embrace social justice, compassion, and grace for all people. Together, we will care for the needy and serve the most vulnerable in our communities.

We declare that our hope is in the Lord Jesus Christ, and that justice in society, and eternal salvation can only be found in Him.

The Kingdom Coalition Manifesto

We, the people of God, declare that it is our responsibility to teach our generation the truths of God's word. The task of the Church is not only the salvation of souls, but also the making of disciples, and lifting up a moral standard for the nations to follow.

We proclaim the warnings of the Bible, that seducing spirits and doctrines of demons will come in the last days. Therefore, we oppose the teachings of Marxism, societal relativism, and intersectionality. It is our responsibility to educate our children about these destructive doctrines and to warn all people of these evils. Socialism produces poverty. Relativism inspires sin and immorality. Intersectionality encourages a destructive, polarizing victim mentality. These teachings will destroy a nation. In the name of Jesus, we renounce them.

We, the people of God, humble ourselves under the mighty hand of God. We bow before Jesus our king and embrace His government in our lives. We receive and look to the ministry of true apostles, prophets, evangelists, pastors and teachers as part of God's government on earth.

We present our lives to God for sanctification and the renewal of our minds so we may be transformed in our thinking and behavior.

We join together as kingdom-of-God people to preach this gospel of the kingdom in all the world. We declare that we are God's family, and we pledge our allegiance to His kingdom.

We, the Church, take a firm stand against social injustice and mob violence. We renounce all anarchistic behavior in America and reject leaders who side with such destructive ways.

We thank God for birthing our nation. We declare that God established our union with the help of great leaders and gave us a divinely inspired Constitution.

We thank Almighty God for the time allotted to us as a nation, for our borders, our flag and our founding fathers. Because America was founded by God on Christian principles, we gladly pledge allegiance to the flag of the United States of America.

We abhor slavery and repent on behalf of the nation for our participation in it. We also cry out against present day social injustice.

Let it be known that we are thankful for our police officers but detest the actions of those who have wrongfully killed unarmed people of color. We call for ongoing racial reform in the nation. We declare our thanks to God for all first responders who serve our communities with valor and godly grace.

We stand in solidarity with all brothers and sisters in Christ, especially those who fear being singled out, abused or killed, when they have done nothing worthy of death. We ask the Lord for safety in our streets, and for grace to remove fear from our minority communities.

We declare that only the Lord Jesus Christ can heal our land, and we embrace Biblical teachings as the only way to reformation and healing in America.

We, the people of God, take our stand against lying Fake news and propaganda. We resist the selective, slanderous bias of evil communication. We expose it as a form of witchcraft and resist its agenda and the evil spirit behind it.

The Kingdom Coalition Manifesto

We resist every political ideology and movement that does not stand for the life of the unborn child, the family, the Church, the poor, social justice for all people and for the support of Israel, who are God's chosen people. We declare that our voting, at government elections, will reflect these values as much as possible.

We declare that poverty is a curse and encourage all political leaders to establish opportunities for all who will work hard so they can prosper financially.

We declare that the truth will set people free. As such, we thank God for our president, our Christian universities and for news networks that communicate truth and promote godly lifestyles.

We thank Almighty God for believers who serve in the political arena, and for believers who report accurate news and influence society for justice and godliness. We thank God for Bible-based education in America at every level, especially in places of higher learning.

We, the people of God, declare that this nation was created for God's eternal purpose. We are deeply concerned about the welfare of America and the advancement of its Christian principles. In that sense, we declare ourselves to be a political people.

We are determined to fight for the blessings of God to remain in America. We follow the example of Jesus who spoke against ungodly leadership in Israel, and we shall do the same in America.

We declare that our help comes from the Lord. We do not rely on the efforts of man to give us salvation or ultimate security.

By God's grace, we aim to take the high ground of government. We will be political and vote for God-inspired leaders who will enact righteous policies and governance.

We proclaim that God has blessed this nation and will continue to bless it in the future. As we will diligently seek the Lord and serve Him, we are assured of His blessings over America for generations to come.

We, the people of God, recognize the three institutions that He has given. They are the family, the Church and civil government.

We declare that, along with the hosts of heaven, the kingdom of God includes these three institutions, and each is called to rule righteously. Each has a God-given authority over their area of influence, and we will strengthen, uphold and pray for them.

We believe in the Biblical model for family: one man, woman and children if they have any. We also understand that a godly family may have only one parent.

We believe in the community of God's holy Church, in spiritual worship, submitting to one another in the fear of God, and in miracles and supernatural answers to prayer.

We declare that the power of God is with us today to perform supernatural signs and wonders. We believe that God is good, His mercies are everlasting and His faithfulness extends to all generations. God's grace and provisions are all we need. We do not frustrate the grace of God but receive His blessings with thanksgiving (see Gal. 2:21).

We will do our part to support and reform each of these three institutions as needed. When any of them violate the designs of heaven, so as to serve the kingdom of darkness, we will not be silent, but will expose the hidden things of darkness, and by God's grace, aim to enact a righteous resolve.

We, the people of God, declare that the Father, Son, and Holy Spirit are One, and that the Lord will one day unify everything under His government.

We declare that the Church is one in Christ. We are one body (see 1Cor. 12) yet we long for the practical manifestation of that unity. We confess that the Church does not yet function as a family, but in time it will.

By God's grace, we humble ourselves, receive His government and come into unity as best we can. Together, we move forward in ministry to see revival in the nations.

We desire the joining of the Lord with other Christians for righteous networking in the body of Christ. We listen for and respond with obedience to God's purpose over America and the nations of the world. We rally together under the banner of Christ.

We declare that the Jewish people are God's chosen people. We agree that the Lord has a unique end-time purpose for them. We bless them and pray for the peace of Jerusalem and for their salvation through Jesus the Messiah. We, the Church, pray for the complete fulfillment of the call of God over the Jews and over the land of Israel.

www.ingramcontent.com/pod-product-compliance
Lightning Source LLC
Chambersburg PA
CBHW071024080526
44587CB00015B/2494